PORTSLADE
A Pictorial History

Commemorative stone bearing the seal of the council on the old fire station.

PORTSLADE
A Pictorial History

Claire Green

Phillimore

1994

Published by
PHILLIMORE & CO. LTD.,
Shopwyke Manor Barn, Chichester, West Sussex

ISBN 0 85033 888 3

Printed and bound in Great Britain by
BIDDLES LTD.
Guildford, Surrey

This book is dedicated to Tricia,
who inspired me to collect old postcards.

List of Illustrations

Frontispiece: Commemorative stone bearing the seal of the council, on the old fire station

Acknowledgements

The author wishes to thank the following: Julian Becher; Peter Cox (Headmaster, St Nicolas' school); Helen Davies (Library and Archives, Cadbury Ltd.); Mr. B. Easey (Registrar, Worthing Registry Office); Bob Gill; Malcolm Hance (General Manager, Rivervale); Peter Lewry; Trevor Meadows (Joint Managing Director, Tates); John Roberts (Brighton and Hove Bus Company); The Salvation Army, Hove; Southern FM Radio; Gordon Smith (Borough of Hove Planning Dept.); Alan Stone (General Sales Manager, Appleyards, Portslade); Linda Brough (European Car Rental); Trevor Povey; Tim Willcox and Isabel Wilson (Hove Museum & Art Gallery); John Younge (Persimmon Homes) and family and friends for their support.

I am indebted to the following who have supplied illustrations for inclusion in the book: Baker & Sons, Portslade, 146; Mrs. Margaret Bryant & Mrs. Dora Reeves, 52, 152, 153; Francis Frith & Co., The Old Rectory, Bimport, Shaftesbury, Dorset, 77, 99, 124, 135; Robert Jeeves, Branch Two, Queens Road, Brighton, 9, 15, 36, 37, 39-41, 46, 47, 54, 57, 63, 69, 70-72, 87, 88, 102, 104, 106-108, 121, 126, 127, 142, 147, 154, 160; Mrs. Irene Marriott & Mrs. Kathleen Ward, 51; Hove Museum & Art Gallery, 2, 4, 5; Trevor Povey, 3, 13, 16, 19, 48, 58, 78, 82, 83, 85, 93, 103, 105, 129, 131-133, 137, 139, 144, 145, 156, 159, 163, 164; Mrs. Patricia Scrivener, 50; Miss Daphne Smith, 38, 43-45; Mrs. Celia Winstanley, 49.

Portslade is a place with a dual character: a veritable 'Dr Jekyll and Mr Hyde' of a place. Portslade Hyde is painfully brutal with its squalid water front and rows of grimy houses and shops, while Portslade Jekyll, a mile from the sea, is a benevolent spot and just as pretty and secluded as nine out of ten of the 'guide-book' villages.

Kipling's Sussex Revisited, R. Thurston Hopkins, 1929

North-east of Kingston about one mile and a half, between two hills, lies the small village of Portslade, between three and four miles from Brighthelmstone; it contains several good houses, and has an old church that cannot boast of much beauty, though it may of antiquity.

Topographical History of Surrey and Sussex, G. L. Gomme, 1900

Portslade, approached by the steepest of roads, is a restful village that has grown an ugly suburb on the sea.

The Sussex Coast, Ian C. Hannah, 1912

Introduction

The parish of Portslade lies on the western boundary of the Rape of Lewes. Hangleton and Aldrington form its eastern boundaries, and it is bordered by Southwick to the west and Poynings to the north. Its southern boundary is formed by the English Channel.

There have been several possible explanations of the name Portslade. The most common theory is that Portslade was the place the Romans knew as *Portus Adurni* (Port of the Adur), being situated at the mouth of the river Adur. Its position would point towards the port and *Lade* signifies a way or passage of waters. Portslade therefore is taken to mean 'the way to the port'. Another variant is that it means 'crossing place of the harbour'. However, *Portus Adurni*, is now thought to have been at Portchester, near Portsmouth, and not Portslade, although there is a strong belief that there was a very important Roman *portus* of some kind near the site of the present Portslade. Doctors Eliot and E. Cecil Curwen interpreted the name to be of Saxon origin as *Portes Lad*, meaning Port's Road. It is commonly agreed that the first component signifies a port, with a further suggestion for the second element being *slaed*, meaning 'shallow valley'.

Spellings of the name vary and it has been *Portes Ladda*, *Portislade*, and appears in Domesday Book as *Porteslamhe*. The Domesday Book entry is the first written record of Portslade, although its origins go back much further. The old gravel pits in Vale Road yielded bones and teeth of the woolly rhinoceros and the mammoth dating from the Ice Age. Stone Age flints and arrow heads were also found and this is the earliest evidence of human habitation in Portslade.

There is a theory that Portslade was the southernmost point of a Roman road from London and it is a fact that a Roman road ran close to the old village. The track came over the Downs from Fulking, round Hangleton Manor and Benfield Manor, down Hangleton Lane and Drove Road and along the lower part of Mile Oak Road where it continued to Southwick. A Roman villa lies under the Methodist church in Southwick Street. It was this road which the Doctors Curwen called Port's Road, being their translation of the Saxon *Portes Lad*.

There is other evidence of Roman settlement in Portslade from the coins and pottery which have been found, and, in 1875, a Roman burial ground was discovered in the brick pits, (now under the recreation ground in Victoria Road) where a large number of funeral urns were unearthed. A complete Castor ware hunt cup with applied decoration representing a hound chasing a deer is on display in Brighton Museum. The cup dates from the late 2nd century and was found in Portslade in 1876. In 1898, Anglo-Saxon graves were discovered at the corner of St Andrew's Road and Church Road, containing three skeletons which were later re-interred in Portslade cemetery.

The church of St Nicolas is of Norman origin with the lower part of the tower dating from *c*.1150. It became the parish church of Portslade in 1368 and the present register dates from 1666, the previous volume having been destroyed. The first entry reads, 'Through the

Sacred Providence of Almighty God the old Church Register of Portslade was burnt by Lightening together with ye Parsonage House of Hangleton on Thursday 31st May between 4 and 6 morning 1666. John Temple, clerke being ye Rector thereof.'

The church is built from flint in the Early English style, and consisted of a nave, chancel and south aisle until 1849 when the north aisle was added. Unlike those of its neighbouring parishes, Portslade parish church has never fallen into total ruin, although in 1686, a survey of parish churches undertaken on behalf of the Bishop of Chichester reported that 'the pulpit had no door and an ill canopy' and that 'the communion cup was battered and cracked'. At the west end of the north aisle is the lavishly decorated chapel and vault of the Brackenbury family of Denton and Sellaby, County Durham, erected in 1869 by Hannah Brackenbury. Hannah Brackenbury had come to Portslade in 1844 and lived at the aptly named Sellaby House. A wealthy and charitable woman, she financed the building of St Nicolas' school in Locks Hill, for the benefit of the poor of Portslade and Hangleton. She died in 1873.

Other notable local families were the Blakers and the Borrers; the Blakers being associated with Portslade since 1485. The earliest documented record of the Blaker family is the will of Edward Blaker, dated 1 October 1571, in which he bequeathes a house and land in Southwick to his son, Edward, and three shillings and fourpence to the poor of Portslade. In her will of 21 February 1578, his wife, Christian, requests that her body be buried in Portslade and she leaves '4 bushells each of wheat and barley' to the poor of Portslade. Kemps, the house at the eastern end of High Street, was built around 1580 and was home to the Blaker family for many generations. Nathaniel Blaker, churchwarden at St Nicolas' in 1764, was one of Portslade's wealthiest citizens. A plaque in St Nicolas' church is dedicated to Harry Blaker (1785-1846), a Brighton surgeon whose firm had the honour of attending Queen Victoria and members of her family. Easthill House was built for Harry's nephew, Edward Blaker, in 1848. The Blaker family vault is outside St Nicolas' church on the south-west corner and bears their coat-of-arms, carved in relief.

William Borrer became Lord of the Manor in 1806, owning half the estate. By 1833, his son, John Borrer, held the whole of the manor and was the principal landowner in Portslade, owning some 1,200 acres. After a tragic life, which included losing two out of three wives in childbirth and the death of six children, John Borrer died in 1866 and his son, Henry, became Lord of the Manor. The grounds of Portslade Manor adjoined St Nicolas' churchyard and a connecting doorway was built into the flint wall. The Borrer family tomb is situated next to this doorway. Inside the church are memorials to two of John Borrer's sons, John and William Arthur. Ten days after his wedding, John, aged 29, was involved in a coach accident at Carlisle on 17 August 1844. Despite 'having endured with remarkable fortitude the amputation of his leg, he died after three days of acute suffering'. The other memorial is dedicated to William Arthur Borrer who 'sailed from Singapore on the 23rd September 1845 and no tiding having been heard of him, it is supposed the vessel foundered in a terrific hurricane which raged in the China seas a few days after he left the port'.

The original Portslade Manor House was built in the 12th century to the north of St Nicolas', with one of its walls forming part of the church boundary. It was a two-storey domestic building of rubble and stone dressings with a later wing constructed from flint with brick dressings. Now ruinous, it is not certain why the building was left to fall into disrepair. The remains were plundered in the 19th century to create a mock ruin, this being a strange practice of the Victorians. Today the ruins are in the grounds of the present Manor House, now St Marye's convent.

In the 1800s, the northern part of the parish consisted solely of downland. Portslade was chiefly a farming community which relied heavily on sheep farming and agriculture. By the mid-19th century Portslade was typical of Sussex downland villages, with thriving farms and market gardens, and the census returns showed that most trades were represented in the population.

In addition to farming and agriculture, Portslade also relied on its other industries. The brewery was established in 1849 by John Dudney and expanded into purpose-built premises in 1881. By 1890, it was capable of producing 1,500 barrels per week of Southdown ale. The Brittania Flour Mills at the southern end of Church Road, the gas works and the electricity works were other important industries, providing valuable local employment. The arrival of the Ronuk factory in Victoria Road in 1902 put Portslade firmly on the map, as the tins of polish took the name all over the world.

Before the arrival of the brewery to Portslade village, water was obtained from a pump in South Street. A piped water supply was laid on to the village in 1879. In 1900, a steam pumping station was built at Mile Oak, which served the whole of Portslade. The gas works were built in 1871, and by 1885, were supplying not only Portslade but the Brighton area also following the closure of the works at Hove and Black Rock. Some twenty years later, in June 1906, the electricity power station was built to the west of the gas works.

Roads were untarred, dirty and dusty. A man with a water cart was employed to walk the streets washing the roads in order to dampen down the dust. In common with other English towns and villages, the early form of transport in Portslade was the horse-drawn vehicle. In the days before motor transport, every landowning family, farmer, shopkeeper and business owned at least one horse and usually several. Ploughs, delivery carts and buses were all pulled by working horses. The horse was heavily relied upon. Portslade Farm in South Street offered its pasture for the convalescence of tired and ailing horses, and Manor Pound at Easthill, owned by Edward Blaker in 1870, provided a similar service.

Where there were horses, there was also the need for a blacksmith. The forge in Foredown Road is over 250 years old and has an adjoining cottage with a smuggler's secret cellar beneath. The coming of the motor vehicle and the introduction of machinery to farms meant that trade for the village blacksmith began to decline. However, Portslade forge was still in regular use until the 1980s, with resident craftsman, Mr. Bill Bowley, making horseshoes.

Windmills were once a common sight in Sussex. Most of the Sussex windmills have long since disappeared, including the two at Portslade. East Hill mill stood on what is now the corner of Mill Close, until it was found to be unsafe and was dismantled around 1880. Copperas Gap windmill was situated in North Street and is known to have existed until at least 1840. The former *Windmill Inn* was built where it once stood. An oil painting, dated 1857 of Southwick Down by David Cox on display in the Marlipins museum, Shoreham, includes both the Portslade windmills in the composition.

Copperas Gap was the area now known as Portslade-by-Sea, and once consisted of just a few fishermen's cottages on the beach. It is possible that it took its name from one of the families who lived in these cottages. The Princess of Wales visited Copperas Gap in 1795 and 'was enlivened by the salubrity of the air'. The coming of the railway to Portslade in 1840 signified the start of Copperas Gap's development into the industrial area we know today. The majority of its houses were built during the 1800s with the district becoming more residential by the end of the 19th century. In 1897, Copperas Gap applied for urban district status which was granted and from then on was known as Portslade-by-Sea.

Portslade old village grew up during the 16th century, with the *Stag's Head* being built about this time and Kemps, its oldest surviving dwelling house, around 1580. By the 19th century, Portslade had become a desirable place to live and many of the large houses, such as Easthill House, Loxdale and Whychcote were built for wealthy families around this time. In 1835, T. W. Horsfield wrote of Portslade: 'The village, which is about four miles from Brighton, contains some good houses, delightfully situated on a declivity of the Downs, and sheltered by their height. The views of the sea are enchanting'. However, because of its position in a hollow, the village was very prone to flooding, a problem which has only been rectified in recent years.

Old Portslade was a typical village with its green, neighbouring farms, church, school and public houses, but whilst this picturesque area was getting a favourable reputation, in contrast, Portslade-by-Sea was developing into a totally unfashionable industrial region, an image that it has unfortunately managed to hold on to. Unless one ventures inland, this part of Portslade is all the motorist sees on his journey along the coast road. Portslade old village was made a Conservation Area in 1974, together with the land to the east of Locks Hill, Easthill Park, South Street and the Manor Road district.

The parishes of Portslade and Hangleton were united in 1864, but separated again in 1951. Portslade Urban District Council was formed on 1 April 1898 and in 1938 consisted of 15 members. Meetings were held at the council chamber, 17 Station Road every second Tuesday in the month. Portslade Town Hall was officially opened on 2 September 1959. Formerly the Ronuk Hall, the building in Victoria Road was purchased at a cost of £36,500. An annexe at the rear was converted into the new council chamber with administration offices and there followed a complete transfer of the council from their old premises in Station Road. A new Local Government Act in 1974 meant that Portslade Urban District Council ceased to exist and Portslade became part of the Borough of Hove.

The 1930s saw the start of land being sold for development. Farms and smallholdings gradually disappeared as housing took over and new estates were built. After the Second World War, much of Portslade's farmland was bought by compulsory purchase orders in order to build much needed housing. Mile Oak, which had previously consisted of only a few dozen houses, suddenly sprang up and many people moved to the area from Portslade-by-Sea. Mile Oak took its name from an old oak tree which used to stand by the roadside, about a mile from the Grange on the western side of the High Street. This rotting tree was a favourite hiding place for children and survived until about 1905.

Whilst on the subject of trees, there is a superstition peculiar to Portslade. The Rev. Henry Hoper, vicar of St Nicolas' from 1815-58, writes:

Singular superstition exists at Portslade near Brighton and has been entertained within the memory of man, namely that a dying person can be recovered if thrice carried round, and thrice bumped against, a thorn of great antiquity, which stands on the Downs, ever ready to dispense its magic power to all believers. A few years ago a medical attendant gave up all hopes of his patient. The Goodies of the village obtained the Doctor's and sick man's consent to restore him to health, and having carried him round the tree bumped the dying man and had the mortification of carrying him back a corpse, much to the astonishment at the ill success of their specific.

(A 'goody' was an old Sussex name applied to an elderly widow.)

Between 1934-36 there were heated objections to a proposed motor-racing track to be constructed on the Downs at Portslade, with an approach road from the Dyke station. The planners had envisaged that the track would be completed during winter 1934-35 and would be a major tourist attraction. Supported by Brighton Council, the Brighton Motor Racing Company Ltd. intended to lay the motor track, enclosed by a five-mile fence, and erect mock Sussex barns at various points along the track to serve as shelters, cloakrooms and lavatories. The noise factor and damage to the beauty of the Downs were the principle objections raised and Portslade Urban District Council rejected the planning applications. The scheme did not go ahead.

One of the more recent changes to affect Portslade in a major way was the widening of the A27 Old Shoreham Road in the 1970s. Many houses, shops and the *Southern Cross* public house were demolished to create a new dual carriageway, approximately double the width of the old road. Road works were completed by 1980, with the speed limit later being raised, somewhat controversially, from 30 to 40 m.p.h.

Portslade has seen many changes and will continue to do so. More buildings will be demolished and replaced, and the surrounding countryside altered as a result of this so-called progress. Through the pictures in this book, let us admire Portslade as it once was, and also appreciate the more modern views, for they too will be history one day.

Early Days

1. The Domesday entry for Portslade. Domesday Book was compiled in 1086 on the instructions of King William I, 20 years after he had conquered England. The purpose of the Survey was to discover how much land the king had, who held it, how many inhabitants were on the land, and its value. As well as being an evaluation of taxes, it became an official register of legitimate ownership of land. A hide was a unit of land usually equal to 120 acres.

Osward ten de Willo PORTESLAGE dim hid. Ipse tenuit T.R.E. 7 ñ geldauit. Iste potuit ire cū tra quo uo luit. Ibi. ē un uilts. Val. VI. solid.

Albtus ten dim hid in PORTESLAMHE. Non geldau. Ibi. ē un uilts cū dim car. Val 7 ualuit. VI. solid.

Osward holds ½ hide [in] PORTSLADE from William. He held it before 1066. It did not pay tax. He could go where he would with the land.
  1 villager.
Value 6s.

Albert holds ½ hide in PORTSLADE. It did not pay tax.
  1 villager with ½ plough.
The value is and was 6s.

2. Copperas Gap, *c*.1816, by W. Scott. Copperas Gap was the name for the area now known as Portslade-by-Sea. The warning beacon was positioned on the cliff top in 1801, amidst fears that Napoleon might invade Sussex. Copperas Gap officially became Portslade-by-Sea in 1897.

3. Copperas Gap windmill was situated in North Street, on the corner of West Street. It survived until at least 1840. The former *Windmill Inn* in North Street was built on the site of the old mill.

4. A view of Portslade in 1840, painted by Henry Earp, senior. This is the earliest known painted view of Portslade which was at that time a small farming community. However, the picture contains much artistic licence. Portslade House, depicted on the hills to the left, is an inaccurate representation, and the vicarage, which was of substantial size, is shown dwarfed against a giant St Nicolas' church.

5. A watercolour by Fred Nash painted in 1841, being the only known picture of Easthill windmill. This post-mill is known to have existed in 1500 as it is mentioned in the will of Richard Scrase, who bequeathed his 'wynde-mylle in Portslade' to his wife Alice. The windmill used to stand on the corner of what is now Mill Close. It was found to be unsafe and was dismantled around 1880.

The Old Village

THE BRIDGE OLD VILLAGE PORTSLADE   182

6.   A much-photographed view, showing the metal footbridge which crossed the High Street and linked the grounds of Portslade House. The metal bridge replaced the original wooden bridge which was set alight by a runaway traction engine in 1885. A smoke deflector is seen positioned underneath the bridge to prevent further misfortunes!
The metal bridge was taken down in 1936 when the Portslade House estate was sold.

7. The western part of High Street as it was *c.*1907. The brick wall and dense trees belonged to the Grange and the cottages further up the hill were known as the Swiss Cottages. George Davey was the publican of the *Stag's Head,* and George Shirer of Shirer's Provision Stores stands outside his shop. The thatched building was the premises of Isaac Holland who, as well as being the publican of the *George Inn*, was a builder, blacksmith, plumber and wheelwright. Known as the Hook and Eye, this building later became the village hall.

8. The same part of High Street but looking eastwards down the hill. It shows the Hook and Eye with its thatched roof, the *Stag's Head* and *George Inn*, the brewery and the Grange on the right. Valley Road now runs where the flint wall once stood. The Swiss Cottages were knocked down *c.*1960 when the road was altered, making it less of a blind corner for motorists turning out of Valley Road. The *George Inn* has been rebuilt and is now the *St George*.

9.   A closer view of the Hook and Eye, the *George Inn* and the Provision Stores (this time under different ownership). The store was owned by Mr. Shirer for two years before Mr. Hammond took over in 1909. Not only was the shop 'noted for best bacon' but it was also very diversely stocked. Items on display outside include saucepans, brooms and bowls, in addition to the groceries for sale.

10.   This picture shows a good view of the Grange, the brewery and the ivy-covered tower of St Nicolas' church, *c.*1915.

11.   The eastern end of High Street, *c*.1912, looking eastwards. A gas lamp is fixed to the brewery wall and beneath it is a fire call box. A switch was pulled inside the box which would connect directly to the fire station and summon help. Read's Supply Stores was owned by Hector Read, who lived in the adjoining house.

12.   The cottages on the opposite side of the road, *c*.1904. A man and boy are sitting on the wall. The Grange can be seen with its chimney smoking, and a horse and cart stands in the road near the corner of South Street.

13. Once called Portslade Street, this is the oldest part of Portslade. The house at the top is Kemps, built around 1580, and is the oldest surviving dwelling in Portslade. It is possible that it was built on St Nicolas' churchyard as there is a 13th-century tomb slab forming part of the kitchen floor. The house was owned by the Blaker family for many generations.

14. Kemps in 1993.

15 & 16.   Once part of Portslade House estate, Portslade Farm was run by Marianne Stallabrass until her death in 1908. At the rear of the farmhouse was the dairy, where butter and milk were produced. Poultry and sausages were also for sale and the farm had grazing land and stables where ailing horses could come to convalesce. The farmhouse still nestles in the corner of South Street by Robin's Row, and is well-known for being home to a family of gypsies for a least twenty years after the Second World War.

17. In the days before a mains water supply served the village, residents had to collect their water from a pump in South Street. Piped water was laid on to the village in 1879, after the brewery had been founded. This photograph shows the remains of the old water pump.

18. A charming view looking down South Street. The large building to the left is Lindfield House, built around 1862. At the bottom of the hill is Portslade farmhouse, and the dense trees in the background are on the Portslade House estate.

19. Three young boys pose by a sewer outlet pipe, or 'stink pole', at the top of Locks Hill and South Street. These pipes were designed to extract methane and other gases from the main sewer which runs under the road here. Manor Lodge can be seen behind the wall, facing the village green.

20. A very rural looking Locks Hill, *c.*1906, before it curves to the left and becomes South Street. The road is rough and untarred. Above the tree tops to the left, the chimneys of Lindfield House in South Street are visible. Behind the sturdy wooden fence is land belonging to Whychcote, which is now the village green.

21.   The village green, Locks Hill, *c*.1935.

Churches

22. St Nicolas' church is of Norman origin and is situated in the heart of Portslade village. It has been the parish church since 1368 and the parish register dates from 1666. The church is built of flint in the Early English style and the lower part of the tower dates from the 12th century. The north aisle was added in 1849, following pleas from the parishioners to have the church enlarged. At the west end of the north aisle there is a lavishly decorated chapel, dedicated to the Brackenbury family, which was erected in 1869 over the family vault by Hannah Brackenbury.

23. This engraving by Richard Henry Nibbs depicts St Nicolas' church in 1851.

24.   The interior of St Nicolas' church.

25.   The United Reformed church (formerly the Congregational church) was built on the site of the Red House, which was a farm until 1896. The church's foundation stone was laid on 25 March 1903 and the church opened for worship, with seating for 200, on 25 June the same year. The original church is now used as the church hall. The present church in Station Road was built on the remaining Red House land in 1932.

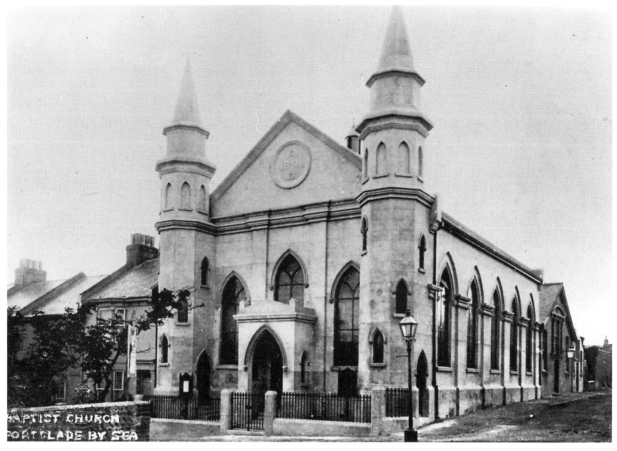

26. The Baptist church in North Street was built in 1891 at a cost of £600. The church was constructed from stone and inside there was a gallery and seating for 450 people. The church membership was cut in the 1950s when many worshippers moved from the area to the new housing development in Upper Portslade. The church in North Street closed in 1959 and was used as a warehouse for some time until its demolition.

27. Today the church and adjoining houses have disappeared and modern warehouses and office buildings stand in their place. The road on this corner is named Chapel Place and serves as a reminder of the old church.

28.   The Baptist church in South Street was built in 1961 to accommodate the growing population of Upper Portslade. The church was erected on the site of Lindfield House.

29.   The Catholic church of Our Lady Star of the Sea and St Denis was erected in 1912 at the expense of Mrs. Denis Broderick of Hove. Together with her husband, Catherine Broderick founded nine churches in all, the last of which was the one at Portslade. The presbytery is also pictured and this too was provided by Mrs. Broderick.

30. The interior of Our Lady Star of the Sea and St Denis was designed in Byzantine style by Nathaniel Westlake. The wrought-iron sanctuary was made by George Greed of Portslade.

31. Interior of Our Lady Star of the Sea and St Denis—the Lady Chapel.

32.   Our Lady Star of the Sea and St Denis in the process of demolition, 28 July 1992. Workmen can be seen removing the tiles from the roof. Church commissioners had decided that the church was 'redundant', in spite of having at least 150 worshippers every Sunday. Despite petitions, the demolition went ahead.

33.   With the church gone, neighbouring St Mary's R.C. Primary School has a brighter aspect and a clearer view down Church Road.

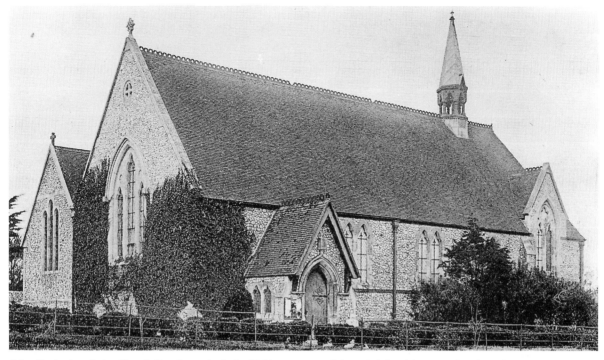

34.   St Andrew's in Church Road was built in 1864, constructed from brick with stone dressings in the Early English style. The designer was Edmond Scott, an architect from Regency Square, Brighton, who also designed the Hannah Brackenbury school in Locks Hill. The parish register dates from 1877. The church was enlarged in 1889 when the north aisle was added and the church now has seating for 525 people.

35.   Portslade cemetery was formed in 1871 on three acres of land. It is divided into three sections: chapel, church (Nonconformist) and Catholic, with two small chapels. The Nonconformist chapel is shown here: it was declared unsafe around the 1940s and is now used as a store. The other chapel is still used for funeral services. Notable graves in Portslade cemetery include the Dudney family; Maria Colwell, the child abuse victim of 1978; and Thomas Huntley Wood, who lived in Ellen Street and was the nautical model for Player's Navy Cut cigarettes.

People and Events

36. A photograph of the Portslade Town Band who were performing under the direction of Bandmaster Hamper, at the Portslade Gas Works Fire Brigade sports on 1 July 1911. Three extra faces have become part of the line up!

37.   Working at the gas works was not all toil. The company organised various social activities for its workers and this photograph shows the Portslade Gas Works Cycle Club. The third annual social of the Gas Works Cycle Club was held in March 1909 where the club captain, Mr. J. Miles, was presented with a case of pipes in honour of his services to the club. The highest number of attendances at runs during the season was achieved by Mr. B. Mepham, whose prize was a cycle lamp.

PORTSLADE
GAS WORKS CYCLE CLUB,

PHOTO

H.W.Tubb

38. 'Some of the B'hoys' were workers from the Brittania Steam Flour Mills. Situated
at the lower end of Church Road, the Brittania Mills were built around 1854 and
originally belonged to John Borrer. Charles Richard Smith & Sons took over the mills
shortly after their erection, which were later owned by Douglas Frederick Sundius Smith
a prominent Portslade figure. The Brittania Mills were demolished in the 1930s.

The B'hoys! PORTSLADE. July. 1923.

39.   With the outbreak of war in 1914, the War Office requisitioned land on which to set up army camps. The camp at Portslade was situated on the football fields of Windlesham House. Loxdale can be seen in the background. Camp Close, at the lower end of Windlesham Close, took its name from the army camp and this area is known locally as the Camp Site.

40.   As Minister of War in 1914, Lord Kitchener appealed for recruits to join the training camps. Men eagerly volunteered to join 'Kitchener's Army', few realising that the war would last so long. This photograph depicts Kitchener's Army Royal Field Artillery in training on the Victoria recreation ground.

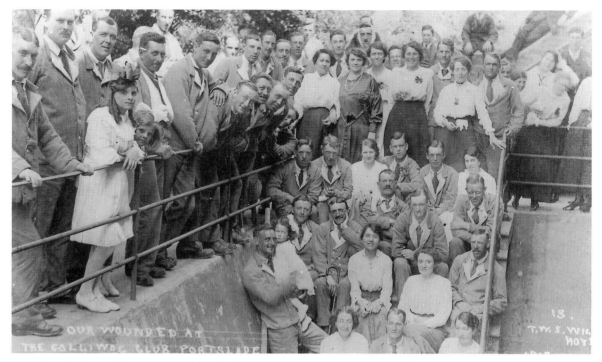

41.   The Golliwog Club was a social club for injured servicemen during the First World War. Entitled 'Our Wounded at the Golliwog Club, Portslade', this photograph of 1917 shows the soldiers, helpers and children on the steps leading down to Portslade Hall, where the meetings were held.

42.   Captioned 'Rest and Peace after War and Work at the Golliwog Club', this photograph shows the men sitting down to tea inside Portslade Hall.

43.   The Portslade amalgamated Sunday Schools before their outing to Hassocks in 1911. The procession passes the parade of shops in Station Road, where Mr. Elliot stands outside his shop, the London Boot Stores. Note the lady watching from a window above Cooper's chemists.

44.   The Portslade-by-Sea Baptist Sunday School follows the Salvation Army band past the *Railway Inn* en route for the station. The united Sunday Schools went by train to Hassocks where they played games, held races, and had a picnic tea in the park.

45. The band of the Salvation Army coming up North Street, leading part of the procession. The Pavilion cinema can be seen on the right. The Salvation Army band was founded by Mr. Albert John Moon in 1896. Mr. Moon was bandmaster until 1929 and is seen here leading the band. He was succeeded by his son, Johnny Moon, who is pictured on the right carrying his cornet. The band broke up in 1969.

46.   Annie Elizabeth White Robinson died on 25 July 1909, aged 21 months, as a result of a scalding accident in her home at 85 St Andrew's Road. The child was lying on the kitchen table whilst being dressed by her mother, and knocked over a saucepan of hot water from a gas-ring on the table. She suffered burns to the front of her body, the right arm and the right thigh. The accident occurred in the afternoon of Saturday 24 July and she died around 10 o'clock Sunday evening. The cause of death was attributed to shock.

47.   The funeral of little Annie Robinson was held on 29 July 1909. She was buried in Portslade cemetery in the Nonconformist section, alongside the hedge. The grave is unmarked. Her father was an adjutant in the Salvation Army and the crowds at the graveside illustrate that the family was well respected.

48. The procession to celebrate the coronation of King George V advances down Station Road in 1911. Huckles furniture store can be seen on the corner of Franklin Road.

49. This photograph was taken in May 1945 outside the Congregational church hall in St Aubyn's Road, where a street party was held to celebrate V.E. Day. The Rev. Stephen Axford, minister of the Congregational church from 1943-47, is pictured standing in front of the Union Jack.

50.   The Portslade Band of Hope on an outing to Maidstone Zoo in 1948. The Portslade branch was formed in March 1927 and was based at the Congregational church, Station Road. Their leader, Grace Robinson, is pictured standing in front of the coach, second from the left. The Band of Hope was a national organisation, formed to deter young people from drinking alcohol.

51. The Portslade Ladies' Lifeboat Guild pictured at their Christmas bazaar at Portslade Town Hall in 1959. The Guild was formed in 1957 by Miss Christine Ford and her parents, Sid and Maud, in order to raise funds for the R.N.L.I. Fund raising included barn dances, bazaars, jumble sales, house to house collections and flag days. Christine Ford is pictured third from right, Sid Ford, centre middle row with Maud standing by the table.

52. St Andrew's Sunday School pose for a photograph in front of the church before setting off on their outing to Hassocks, 10 July 1923.

53. Controlled by the council, Portslade-by-Sea fire brigade was very poorly equipped, having only hand-carts with which to attend fires. With such limited equipment, the capabilities of the brigade were restricted, and thus for larger blazes they combined forces with the Portslade Gas Works fire brigade. A motorised appliance was not purchased until 1927. Prior to the fire station being built in 1909, the hand-carts and other equipment were stored at the council yard, Trafalgar Road. The brigade is pictured here, c.1907. On the left is Second Officer, Fred Puttock, who became Officer-in-Charge around 1929. The firemen are pictured wearing berets, which were part of the uniform up until the Second World War, but they donned brass helmets when fighting fires.

Schools

54. St Nicolas' School was built in 1872 on the east side of Locks Hill, the architect being Edmund Scott, who also designed St Andrew's church. A tablet in the wall denotes 'These schools were erected by Hannah Brackenbury for the benefit of the poor of the United Parishes of Portslade and Hangleton'. There were separate departments for girls, boys and infants. The infants moved to a new building in 1903, followed by the transfer of the boys' school in 1924, which left the girls' school occupying the Brackenbury building. This postcard is captioned 'St Nicolas' Girls' School'. In 1929, the girls' school merged with the infants and became mixed junior and infants. It is now the annexe of the Portslade County Infants' School and caters for second-year pupils.

55. St Nicolas' Infants' School, on the west side of Locks Hill, with a group of teachers posing outside. The school opened on 23 July 1903. In 1924, it became St Nicolas' Boys' School and later the St Nicolas' Senior Boys' School when the schools were reorganised in 1929. It is now Chimneys, East Sussex County Council's family consultation centre.

56. The foundation stone for the St Nicolas' Church of England Junior School was laid by the Secretary of the Church Assembly on 7 June 1963. Built at a cost of £70,000, the new school was opened by the Bishop of Lewes, the Rt. Rev. J. H. Morrell, on 12 July 1967. The mural was designed by John A. Guillam Scott and depicts St Nicholas, the patron saint of children.

57. The first St Andrew's public elementary school was erected in 1881. It catered for children of all ages until 1906 when the infants were transferred to the newly-built St Peter's School. St Andrew's was condemned in 1911 and a decision was made to rebuild the school. Financing the project relied heavily on public donations. This photograph shows work in progress.

58. Captioned 'New School, Portslade-by-Sea', this photograph shows St Andrew's School after rebuilding. Building work cost £5,000. The school reopened on 25 April 1914, with the ceremony being performed by the Bishop of Chichester. It was constructed on two floors with 13 classrooms, and could now hold 650 children. The classrooms were designed so that each could be opened to form one large hall. Another unusual feature was the fact that the playground was on the roof! Reorganisation of the schools in 1929 meant that St Andrew's became mixed junior and senior girls, the juniors being taught downstairs and the seniors upstairs. The school was sold to Kayser Bondor in 1948 and the children were transferred to Benfield School on the Old Shoreham Road.

59.   Portslade House stood in 40 acres of ground, which stretched down to the Old Shoreham Road. The house and 27 acres of ground were purchased in 1913 by Mrs. Scott Malden, the principal of Windlesham House School, a Brighton preparatory school for boys, which was moving to Portslade. Mrs. Scott Malden chose to live in Portslade House and a new school was built next to it. This opened on 27 September 1913. In 1935, Windlesham House and its grounds were up for sale as the school was on the move again. Portslade Urban District Council failed in their attempts to acquire the building and grounds for use as council offices and a public park. Windlesham House was purchased by the vicar of Portslade and remained a school. It is now the Portslade Community College sixth form department. Portslade House was demolished c.1936 and its grounds sold for house building.

60.   The chapel at Windlesham House School was originally the old Carfax church at Oxford, demolished in 1896. Mrs. Scott Malden purchased and rebuilt the church as a chapel for her Brighton school. The chapel was dismantled and moved to the new school at Portslade where it was reconstructed.

61. The Industrial School was founded in 1902 by London County Council. Situated in its own grounds, its position was described in *Kelly's Directory* of 1918 as 'commanding a sea view extending from the Isle of Wight to Beachy Head'. The institution had room for up to 120 pupils. Those admitted had either committed a crime and were too young to be imprisoned or were unmanageable at home. The boys, mostly from London, learnt various skills, such as carpentry and gardening, and the school had its own band. An observer wrote: 'the lads wear green sweaters, cord trousers and are hatless working in the garden'. In 1909, the London County Council's inspector reported that the school was achieving good results but that it was 'a pity that an institution specially designed for the work should have so many empty places.' In 1911, the school had 109 occupants. The Industrial School later became known as the Mile Oak Approved School, nicknamed the 'Naughty Boys' School'.

62. The stone statue which used to be above the main entrance to the Industrial School, now in the grounds of Foredown Tower. The Latin inscription *lex dei lux viae*, translates to 'the word of God lights the way'.

63. Taken from the Downs, this photograph shows the Senior Girls' School, Mile Oak, now part of Portslade
Community College. Chalky Road, Graham Avenue and surrounding streets are yet to be built and Valley Road can be
seen under construction. The school was built *c*.1940 and its first pupils were the senior girls from St Andrew's School,
which had closed on the outbreak of war.

Leisure and Recreation

64.   The Paddocks were 39 acres of pleasure grounds, with tea gardens, a model farm and stables for breeding and training racehorses. The 1908 Derby winner, *Signorinetta*, owned by Chevalier Ginistrelli, is rumoured to have been trained at the Paddocks. There were facilities for playing football, tennis, bowls, cricket and croquet and, as this picture shows, tobogganing.

65.   This picture shows some of the animals at the Paddocks model farm. Behind the fence, the visitors are sitting down for afternoon tea in the enclosure. It was a very popular place. To the right, two ladies are standing by a large urn, in front of which is a black kettle. The tea was brewing!

66.   An overall view of the Paddocks, showing several farm wagons in the fields. Note the long building which has 'TEA GARDENS. Tennis. Croquet. Bowls. Cricket' painted on the roof. On the left there is a sign saying 'Football' and to the right is another hatch where people are queuing. Something is painted on the wall but the hatch is open and the letters are obliterated. It is thought to say 'Quoits'.

67.   A similar view is shown here. Portslade Paddocks are shown on a map of 1899 as being on the east side of what is now Mile Oak Road, near to where the parade of shops is today. The last remaining buildings of the Paddocks went up for sale by auction in 1935. Foxhunters Road, Sefton Road, Beechers Road, and Paddock Court all take their names from Portslade Paddocks' racing connections. The Mile Oak Road can be clearly seen in this picture.

68 & 69. The Victoria recreation ground lies on the site of the old brick pit where, in 1875, a Roman burial ground was discovered and a large number of funeral urns were found. The park was officially opened on 11 August 1902, as a finale to other festivities celebrating the coronation of King Edward VII. Note the layout of the park with paths, steps and benches. There were once two ornate wrought-iron shelters with stained glass windows, one of which is shown in the photo below, which dates from c.1911.

70.   The Queen's Nurses fête held in the Victoria recreation ground on Whit Monday, 27 May 1912. The event was to raise funds for the local Queen's Nurses and it attracted large crowds. The Mayoress of Hove performed the opening ceremony, which was preceded by a procession led by the Portslade Town Band. A display of drill, dancing and singing by the combined schools of Portslade followed the speeches. There was a lengthy and varied programme of events which included displays, sports competitions, stalls and sideshows.

71. The Portslade Gas Works fire brigade sports day, 1 July 1911. This was an annual event held on their own recreation ground. The crowd is watching the fun in front of the officers' lavatory. The highlight of the event was the individual championship, involving various drills, which was won for the fourth time by Fireman A. Eastwood, who became the first holder of the new silver Challenge Cup.

FIRE BRIGADE COMPETITION WET DRILL
PORTSLADE GAS WORKS SPORTS.

WILES BROS.

72. Other events included an inter-brigade four-men horse-cart drill, in which nine Sussex brigades took part. There were also competitions for the home brigade, and entertaining events such as the bolster fight on a greasy pole over a tank of water. This picture shows the wet drill competition. A fireman demonstrates his hose skills whilst the rest of the crew pump the water from the trough.

73. The second annual sports day of Hove College, 15 July 1914. The event was held on the paddock, Hillbrow, Portslade, by kind permission of the owner, Mr. H. R. Hornby. The Southwick Town Band provided musical entertainment for the 200 spectators. The Industrial School can be clearly seen in the background.

74 and 75. Ronuk Ltd. regularly launched puzzle competitions, with monetary prizes. These competitions were extremely popular, having several hundred prize winners. A favourite type of puzzle is illustrated here, together with the solution. The idea was to unscramble the words and phrases and paste them together to form an advertisement; a somewhat difficult task considering there were no clues as to the wording of the advertisement.

RESULT of the
RONUK
£1,000 Family
PUZZLE COMPETITION

BY APPOINTMENT TO H.M. THE KING.

RONUK
POLISHES

not only produce a richness of polish, but a sense of cleanliness and satisfaction which nothing else can equal.

Buy full value.

RONUK POLISHES, PRESERVES & PURIFIES FLOORS, WOODWORK, LINO, FURNITURE, LEATHER, LACQUERED METALS, Etc.

QUICK, EASY TO USE & LONG LASTING.

USE THE BEST OF POLISHES FOR ECONOMY AND A BRIGHT & HEALTHY HOME.

COLRON
WOOD DYES

RONUK FLOOR & WOODWORK STAINS

Ordinary bare wood floors or any new woodwork made to look like polished oak or other hard woods.

The most decorative stains ever made. Cannot wear off. Easy to apply. Ideal for woodworkers.

The above is reproduced from a photograph of the "RONUK-COLRON" advertisement as originally drawn and forms the "key" to the puzzle

1st Prize - £60

Won by

MRS. E. WALKER
31, Wellington Hill West, BRISTOL 7
(Area No. 5)

(For full list of 1000 Awards, see inside)

RONUK LTD. · PORTSLADE · SUSSEX

"By far the Best"

Buildings

76. Benfield Manor, or Benfields, from a woodcut, copied from James Lambert Junior's drawing of 1782. Benfields was an old hunting lodge, situated near Hangleton Manor and built in the 14th century. It was owned originally by the Benfield family and subsequently owned by the Coverts, one of the most wealthy landowning families of the time. The building was constructed from flints and brick plinths, with a 66ft.-wide frontage. The porch, window-frames and doorway were of stone and the door was oak panelled. Over the doorway and windows were rows of armorial shields. Benfields later became ruinous and was demolished in 1871 to make way for cottages for Benfield Farm. Some of the shields were saved and inset into a garden wall at Easthill House, but this wall no longer stands.

77. Easthill House was built by Edward Blaker in 1851 in 750 acres of land, the remainder of which now forms Easthill Park. It was home to the Blaker family for many years and also to John Dudney, the owner of the brewery. The house was sold to Portslade Urban District Council in July 1947 to use as a community centre, and the grounds became a public park. Easthill House was threatened with demolition in 1964 but was reprieved. It now belongs to East Sussex County Council and houses the Portslade toy library.

78.   The Grange was built *c*.1770 for the bailiff of the Portslade House estate. It stood in the High Street, opposite today's entrance to Valley Road. Its grounds stretched to the corner of South Street and were enclosed by a high brick wall. The frontage of the Grange appears in many photographs of the old village but it is rare to see the house from the rear as in this photograph. The Grange was demolished *c*.1930.

79.   Whychcote was built in the late 1880s for Herbert Mews, then the co-owner of the brewery. This grand three-storey Victorian house was built with nine bedrooms, three bathrooms, five cellar rooms and had extensive grounds and tennis courts. In 1928, it was bought by Andrew Melville, proprietor of the Grand Theatre, Brighton, who lived there until his death in 1938.

80. Loxdale was built in 1899, on land owned by John Hall of Portslade House, for Walter Mews, brother of Herbert. Walter Mews died in 1922 and his widow lived at the house until 1928, when it was sold and became a 'Home for Little Boys'. During the Second World War, the building was used by the army, and the top floor was set alight by incendiary bombs during an air raid. In 1946, Loxdale was bought by London County Council to house boys from the Industrial School. It was later purchased by Lewisham County Council and used as a children's home; an old people's holiday home; and an approved school for girls. It has been owned by the Swedish Folk High School since 1979.

81. The original Portslade Manor House dated from the 12th century, the ruins of which are in the grounds of the present Manor House, built in 1807. In 1904, the Manor House was sold to the nuns of the Poor Servants of the Mother of God, and became St Marye's convent. Their benefactor was a Miss Kathleen Nelson, who is buried in the convent grounds. The chapel, added later, can also be seen in this photograph.

82. A photograph of St Marye's convent, taken from inside the grounds, *c.*1909, showing a statue of the Blessed Virgin Mary. St Marye's is now a home for mentally retarded women who are educated and cared for by the nuns.

83. Hillbrow was the home of the Stallabrass family. Marianne Stallabrass, who ran Portslade Farm, was the last of the family to live in the house and can be seen here in the doorway. The house comprised four large bedrooms, bathroom, two substantial reception rooms, with stabling, greenhouses, gardens and an orchard. After Marianne died, the house was auctioned. The *Sussex Daily News* of 28 July 1909 reports: 'There was a large attendance at the *Old Ship Hotel*, Brighton yesterday afternoon, when Messrs. Young, Holbech and Sadler of Second Avenue, Hove and Station Road, Portslade submitted the valuable and compact freehold country house or small pleasure farm, known as Hillbrow, Upper Portslade, consisting of a superior modern built bungalow residence, with land amounting to nearly seven acres. The bidding started at £1,100 and advanced to £1,725, at which price it was withdrawn. The property is now open for disposal by private treaty'. Hillbrow was demolished *c.*1960 and Rowan Close built on the site.

84. Originally known as Hangleton Hospital, Hove Sanatorium opened in 1883, admitting patients with infectious diseases. It was built for Hove Commissioners, predecessor of Hove Borough Council, on a six and a half acre site, and was approached by a long country lane. Its position was considered high enough for the patients to benefit from the fresh air and remote enough to minimise the risk of infection, hence the name the Foredown Isolation Hospital, as it later became known. This photograph shows Block A, the tuberculosis ward. The advancement of modern medicine meant that infectious diseases were less prevalent and, by the 1970s, the hospital was no longer admitting patients. It became a hospital for handicapped children but finally closed in 1988. The site was sold for property development and the hospital was demolished.

85. The water tower was built in 1909 to supply the Foredown Isolation Hospital which was then undergoing extension and improvement. The cast-iron tank was made by J. Every of Lewes and when full contained 156.6 tonnes of water. The walls of the tower were brick-built to a thickness of up to 33 inches, in order to withstand the immense pressure. By 1972, the isolation hospital had closed and the water tower was no longer used.

86. When Persimmon Homes purchased the site of the former hospital, the water tower was included in the deal. It was subsequently sold to Hove Borough Council in September 1990 who have restored and converted it into a countryside centre. The main attraction is a camera obscura housed in the old water tank, where the ballcock is still in place. The new-look Foredown Tower opened to the public on 13 July 1991.

37. The *Railway Inn* celebrates the coronation of King George V in 1911. The *Railway Inn*, later known as the *Railway Tavern* and now the *Railway Hotel*, is known to have been a public house since at least 1882. Note the cottage to the right with the crooked chimney, which formed part of the original Portslade railway station. These cottages were later demolished and public conveniences built on the site.

88.   The Portslade Corps of the Salvation Army was formed on 2 August 1882. Meetings were held in a building in Albion Street which used to be the parish church school. By 1909, the Portslade Corps had 120 members and the school building was considered inadequate. A new citadel was to be built almost opposite their existing headquarters on the corner of North Street, on land donated by Messrs. Frederick Sundius Smith and Richard Smith of the nearby Brittania Flour Mills. Six foundation stones were laid at the ceremony on 27 August 1910 by Walter Hillman (Chairman of the Portslade Urban District Council), Mrs. E. J. Parker, The Assistant Chief Secretary, Ernest Clevett, Jasper Colwell and one on behalf of Richard Smith who could not be present. Three of the stones are seen here in position.

89.   The new Salvation Army citadel on the corner of North Street. The building had accommodation for 300 adults plus adjoining officers' quarters. The Salvation Army ceased to use the citadel in October 1966 and it is today used by a firm manufacturing grates and fireplaces.

90.   The fire station in Church Road opened on 3 November 1909. On either side of the main entrance are commemorative stones bearing the seal of the council, which were inset during the opening ceremony. On the first floor were the Chief Officer's room and the recreation room, with a sliding pole to the engine house below. The Portslade-by-Sea fire brigade, controlled by the local council, consisted of retained firemen. A system was installed at the fire station whereby every fireman received the emergency call at his home at the same time as the street alarm was raised. After the Second World War, the fire service became nationalised. The building ceased to be used as a fire station in 1948 and the Portslade-by-Sea brigade was absorbed with Hove. Since then, the old fire station has been an antiques warehouse, a builder's premises, and it now belongs to Freeway Tools and Fixings, who purchased it in June 1988.

91.   The police in Portslade came under the authority of the Portslade Watch Committee. The police station in St Andrew's Road was built *c*.1909 to replace the county police station at the west end of North Street. In 1919, it was occupied by Superintendent W. Suter and three constables. The police cottages, still standing today, were sited between nos. 67 and 69 St Andrew's Road.

92.   Portslade Town Hall in Victoria Road was originally the Ronuk Memorial Hall, built in 1927 as a social centre for the factory workers. Council matters had previously been conducted at Portslade Hall, no. 17 Station Road, at the rear of the Vine and Lee garage. After the Ronuk factory closed, their hall was purchased by the council at a cost of £36,500. The old council offices had become inadequate and it was felt that the people of Portslade needed a social centre. The new Town Hall was officially opened by the Chairman of the Council, Councillor Robert Shields, on 2 September 1959.

Streets

93.   Church Road, Portslade, *c.*1915. The entrance to St Peter's Road is on the left. The shop at no. 17 was owned by Mr. Charles Sleeman and had a doorway knocked through from the shop to the front room of no.15, next door. In the late 1930s, the new occupants of no.15 had this doorway blocked up when they found that old Mr. Sleeman, who was still living above his old shop, was asleep in their front room!

94. The southern end of Church Road, *c.*1904, facing the Brittania Flour Mills. The road narrows at the end and leads into Wellington Road, where the *Crown Inn* is visible.

95.   Looking westwards along St Andrew's Road, c.1917. The houses were built in the late 1890s. A horse-drawn bus
s approaching behind the man walking towards the camera. The pavements appear to be a recent addition as hardly
anyone is using them. Old habits die hard and people were used to walking in the road.

96.   The west side of this thoroughfare is Station Road, Portslade but the east side is Boundary Road, Hove. This
picture looks north towards the railway station and the gabled building behind the tree is the *Railway Inn.* Crossing over
into Boundary Road, the shop second from the right belongs to Harold Wright, a furniture dealer, who has some of his
wares on the pavement.

97. Looking south from Portslade station, *c.*1900. The houses adjacent to the *Railway Inn* have now been pulled down and the pavements widened to create a parade of shops. Note the delightful horse-drawn bus.

98. The bottom end of Station Road/Boundary Road, *c.*1909. The writing on the side wall of no. 12 Boundary Road advertises the business of Walter Hillman, corn merchant, hay and straw dealer, and general carting contractor. Between this building and that which juts out behind is the entrance to Seaford Road.

99.   Station Road/Boundary Road in the 1950s. The fruit and vegetable stall is on the corner of North Street. The wall of the house advertises the offices of H. Baker, timber importers and builders' merchants, at 77 North Street. The sign behind the man reads 'To the Pavilion Cinema' where *A Date with Judy* is being shown. Note the difference between the street lighting; tall poles with scroll-work on the Portslade side, but shorter lamp standards on the Hove side. The entrance to Seaford Road is on the right.

100.   A leisurely scene in Trafalgar Road, *c*.1905. On the right is Coustick's the bakers; their delivery cart can be seen just setting off. The manure in the road is a reminder of the days before motor traffic! The shop of Henry Broomfield, pork butcher, can be seen on the left.

101.   Trafalgar Road, *c*.1915. Arthur Charles Inskipp's draper's shop is on the left, selling gents' hosiery, caps, shirts, pants and vests. James S. Hills has a grocer's shop next door and also a tobacconist's in the adjacent premises. A fire call post can be seen at the kerb, and the cart in the road belongs to Henry Brundle, a greengrocer in Abinger Road.

102.   A view of North Street which is almost unrecognisable today. On the left, the building with the round windows is the old Pavilion cinema, formerly known as the Picturedrome, whilst the Baptist church can be seen a little further along. Alongside the Salvation Army citadel, a poster advertises a performance by the Eastbourne Band.

103.   North Street, *c*.1922. On the right is the shop belonging to George Ariss, general draper and outfitter. The women and children are standing outside the premises of Walter Long, watchmaker and jeweller.

104.   Old Shoreham Road looking westward, *c.*1930. The dense trees are on land belonging to the Portslade House estate which extended north to High Street. With only four motor vehicles using the road, it is a far cry from today's busy dual carriageway.

105.   Old Shoreham Road, *c.*1924, viewed from just west of Locks Hill. It is hard to believe this is the same road today. No. 147 is the shop of W. Hughes, baker, confectioner and corn merchant; the shop also served teas and refreshments. All these buildings were demolished in the early 1970s.

106. Southern Cross in the 1920s showing the *Southern Cross* public house on the corner and St Nicolas' Infants'
School. The *Southern Cross* closed on 3 November 1973 before it and the adjoining houses were demolished for road
widening. A lady is chatting to a milkman, whose cart bears the wording 'Cherryman. Dairy'. Michael Cherryman ran
the dairy at no. 2 Gordon Road, Portslade, and sold milk from the churn on the cart. Measuring jugs can be seen
hanging on the side.

107.   Looking down Carlton Terrace, *c.*1920. The *Railway Inn* and station can be seen at the end of the road, with a steam train passing through. The houses on the right have now lost their front gardens and have been converted into shops.

108.   Norway Street has changed little since this photograph was taken. The poster on the left reads 'Use only Rose Metal Polish & Boot Shinium Polish'. In the 1920s, the Rose Metal Polish Co. Ltd. had premises in Symbister Road and later in Victoria Road, when they were known as Rose Polishes Ltd.

Twittens and Lanes

109.   This picture depicts what is now Foredown Road in the early 1900s. The postcard was posted in Portslade on 10 June 1919. It reads: 'Thank you so much for writing. I am pleased to hear Mrs. Carter is better, by this perhaps she is home again. Mother and I are staying with my brother and thoroughly enjoying our visit—we motor somewhere every day! Do send me Shelagh's snap shot—glad the dear child is so happy. She will be sorry to leave the Farm. My love to her. Yrs. Sister Flower.' Sister Flower gives her holiday address as 'Alma Cottage, Upper Portslade'. Alma Cottage is in South Street and stands almost opposite the Baptist church. *Pike's Directory* of Brighton of 1919 lists a Sidney Emery as being the occupier of Alma Cottage. It seems likely that Mr. Emery, who lived there for several years, was Sister Flower's brother with whom she was staying.

110.   The same section of Foredown Road today, as one goes up the hill from Drove Road. Drove Road is considered to be on the site of a Roman road, known as Port's Road, which ran over the Downs from Fulking and through Hangleton, Portslade and Southwick.

111 & 112. *(Left and below left)* When the railway line from Brighton to Shoreham opened in May 1840, bridges were built over the railway and tunnels constructed underneath in order to facilitate access. The cattle arch is one such tunnel, being part of an ancient thoroughfare. Cattle were driven from the Downs, following a southerly route down under the railway line (hence the name 'cattle arch') into Gordon Road, along the twitten leading into Station Road, and on to the slaughterhouses in North Street. The drovers' route today would have started from the Downs, gone along the bridle path at the back of Brasslands Drive, down through the village into Locks Hill, round the back of St Nicolas' School, along the Old Shoreham Road, down past Benfield School, through the cattle arch, along the twitten into Station Road, and thence to North Street. The lighting in the tunnel is a recent addition to improve the safety of pedestrians.

113. *(Below right)* The twitten between Gordon Road and Station Road, part of the old drovers' route.

114. The shady lane to Easthill, c.1931. The opening on the right is the entrance to Easthill Park.

15. The same view today, the road now being Easthill Way. The flint wall and part of the wall in the distance can till be recognised, although the road itself has widened quite considerably.

Portslade-by-Sea

THE ORIGINAL & GENUINE COPYRIGHT PORTSLADE-BY-SEA CREST.
(P. J. W. BARKER'S COPYRIGHT)

MEANING OF THE CREST: -
AT THE TOP: –

A Roman Galley, signifying the ancient Roman Origin of Portslade, when it was called "Portus Adurni" meaning, "The Port of the Adur". Near here John landed after the death of Richard I and Charles II embarked after the Battle of Worcester.

In the left hand top quarter: –
A Cornucopia or "Horn of Plenty" signifying the local industry of market gardening.

In the right hand top quarter: –
The Six Sussex Martlets, so long associated with Sussex.

In the lower left hand quarter: –
A Bunch of Grapes signifying "Health"

In the lower right hand quarter: –
An Oak branch signifying "Strength"

The Latin Motto "Vive Valeque"
which being freely translated means "Here's health and strength to you".

PORTSLADE HAS BEEN FAMOUS FOR HEALTHINESS FOR OVER 100 YEARS
vide "Brighton Herald" Aug. 14th 1819 & Aug. 16th 1919.

On several occasions it has had the lowest death rate in the kingdom.

Each piece of the genuine crest china has printed upon it the words Copyright P. J. W. Barker, Portslade.

The entire crest designed by P. J. W. Barker, 110 & 112 Trafalgar Rd. Portslade–by–Sea.

116. The Portslade-by-Sea crest, designed *c.*1920 by P. J. W. Barker, who owned a drug store and tobacconist's at nos. 110 and 112 Trafalgar Road. The Roman galley is said to signify the Roman origin of Portslade; the cornucopia signifies its main industry of market gardening; six Sussex martlets; grapes meaning health and an oak branch signifying strength. The motto means 'health and strength'.

117. In 1903, Portslade beach was described as follows: 'The beach at Portslade is admirably adapted for bathing and free from the vast accumulation of shingle that makes bathing so uncomfortable in many neighbouring towns'. Looking at this photograph, taken around the same time, with the seaweed and the pebbles, it is difficult to see the beach in the same favourable light!

18.   Portslade beach, *c.*1909. There appears to be a boys' school outing as several of the boys are dressed alike. Note the girl with the ribboned pigtails wearing what appears to be a knotted handkerchief on her head, standing close to her little brother.

119. The canal at the bottom of Station Road/Boundary Road. The *Halfway House* public house can be seen in the background. At one time there was a refreshment hut run by the ferryman and his wife. For a fare of one penny, the ferry would take up to six people at a time across the canal to the beach, and it can be seen here with three passengers. The ferry was in operation until the 1960s.

120. Most of the buildings shown in the previous picture have now gone, as have the ferry and the beach. The *Halfway House* remains and the buildings along the Kingsway have hardly changed.

121. The ferry station and gas works, *c.*1912. John Eede Butt & Sons' timber-yard can be seen to the right, as can the electricity works.

122. A general view of the canal at Portslade, looking west. The electricity works can be seen across the water. A cart drawn by two heavy horses is making its way along the path. Note the steep flight of steps leading up to Wellington Road. At the top of the steps is the *Jolly Sailors* public house.

123. The canal at Portslade showing the electricity works with the gas works a little further to the east. The cottage was known as Crab Cottage, or Crab House, named after the little shop next door which used to sell crabs and other seafood.

124.   Wellington Road in the 1950s. The *Crown Inn*, opposite the bottom of Station Road, was one of the oldest inns in Portslade, being built around 1840. Once the haunt of smugglers, it had extensive underground cellars and a gallery which looked out over the water. The *Crown Inn* was demolished in 1969. The timber-yard of John Eede Butt at Baltic Wharf is being advertised on the building behind.

Transport

125.   Portslade station *c*.1926, shortly before it was renamed 'Portslade and West Hove' in 1927. Owned by the London, Brighton & South Coast Railway, the station opened on 12 May 1840. It closed in July 1847 and did not reopen until October 1857, on a different site. The two railway cottages which formed part of the original station were later demolished and replaced by public conveniences. On the side of the station building is painted 'Robins Ltd. Wine Merchants & Beer Bottlers, 79 Boundary Rd.' A horse-drawn cart waits outside the station entrance.

26.   Station Approach, *c.*1920. The *Victoria Hotel* is pictured on the corner of Victoria Road. The crossing gates are
 osed and a pedestrian, motor-car and horse-drawn cart are waiting for the train to pass through. There was a wicket
 ate either side of the railway line so that pedestrians could cross whilst the train was in the station. The manual
 ossing gates were removed in the late 1960s and automatic barriers installed.

127.   The Portslade to Kemp Town bus, a Milnes-Daimler CD436 owned by the Brighton, Hove and Preston United Omnibus Company, waits outside Portslade station, *c*.1909. This service later became Route no.1 from Portslade station which terminated at Arundel Road, Kemp Town.

128.   Service 1A waits at the Fishersgate terminus at the end of Eastbrook Road in 1927. The bus is a Tilling-Stevens TS3A sporting pneumatic tyres which were introduced to new vehicles that year. From Fishersgate, the bus would travel to Sussex Square, Brighton via Franklin Road, New Church Road and Western Road. Service 1A was introduced on 19 May 1927 but was withdrawn, after only 17 months, on 3 October 1928. It was replaced by Service 6.

129. There were three steam-roller accidents in the High Street. Two vehicles came to grief whilst going up the hill and one whilst coming down. This was probably due to the fact that their wheels had no grip. If the driver was in the wrong gear whilst negotiating the hill and the engine lost momentum, he would lose control of the vehicle and overturn. This photograph shows the fate of a steam-roller which was travelling up the hill *c.*1905.

130. A no. 15 Southdown bus, from Portslade to Hollingbury, passes the company's central works in Victoria Road in the 1950s. The Portslade works were built in 1928 for petrol-electric vehicles and incorporated a chassis shop, body shop, paint shop, signwriters, engine shop and test house, blacksmith and tinsmith, electricians, clothing shop and stores. The company held an annual open day where the public could visit the Portslade works.

Upper Portslade and Mile Oak

131. This photograph dates from around 1916 and shows the houses in North Road and Southdown Road. The land in the foreground belongs to North House Farm, and is where Valley Road was later built. The brewery is prominent as is the oast house, dating from 1849, which formed part of the original brewery at Portslade.

132. North House Farm and the Stonery market gardens, c.1914. Foredown Hospital and the water tower can be seen on the skyline. North House Farm and Stonery Gardens were owned by John Broomfield, who also owned Mile Oak Farm. North House Farm was demolished around 1947. The photograph was taken from where Drove Crescent is today and Valley Road now runs through the middle of the picture.

133.   This photograph was taken in the 1920s from 'Lover's Lane', the twitten off Foredown Road. The gate would now lead into the playing fields at Peter Gladwin School. The Industrial School can be seen on the skyline and to the right is the school caretaker's cottage. The line of trees marks the position of Valley Road today.

134.   Mile Oak Road in the 1920s. Next to the bungalow on the left are the Royal Tea Gardens. Frederick Stallabrass owned the tea gardens at no.105 Mile Oak Road in the 1920s and '30s. Brasslands Drive, named after the Stallabrass family, has now been built between the tea gardens and the large house. Dennis Stallabrass was the owner of the first motor-car in Portslade and Marianne Stallabrass ran Portslade Farm.

135.   Taken from Mile Oak Road, *c*.1953, this photograph shows the Downs before development. The fence posts today stand outside Wickhurst Rise flats. The white hut marks the position of Portslade sports centre and Chalky Road now runs to the left. The bus stop was for Service 15B, which served Mile Oak Road from December 1943 to May 1963.

136.   This photograph, taken in 1991, shows the same section of the Downs and illustrates how the land has been heavily utilised for building. The sports centre can be seen where the white hut was located.

137. Mile Oak in the 1930s. Mile Oak Road runs through the middle of the photograph and the chimney of the water-works can be seen. The cluster of sheds and farm buildings belong to Wrapson's nurseries. In the centre, backing onto the downland, are the bungalows of Chrisdory Road. Graham Avenue has not been constructed and the reservoir can be seen in the background.

138. Unrecognisable today, this picture shows the lower part of Mile Oak Road in the 1920s. Mile Oak Gardens now runs through where the wall on the left stands.

Trade

139. Hector Read's Supply Stores in High Street, c.1920, which sold just about everything. Note the carcasses hanging outside. All the available space was used for the display of goods. Above the bay window are numerous pots and pans, a wicker laundry basket, a tin bath, a trunk, mats and a pan stand with different sized saucepans. A crate is being hoisted by pulley to the upper floor.

140. When the building next door was altered to a café (now a model shop), its new frontage protruded and thus obscured Read's advertising on the wall. The writing was repainted on the remaining upper section. Read's Supply Stores no longer trades but the advertising on the wall remains.

141. The music shop of Rex Camps & Co. at no. 44 Station Road, *c.*1935. Camps were sole agents for 'His Master's Voice' radios and stocked a large range of musical instruments, gramophone records and sheet music. The shop has been extended and is now the Seeboard showroom.

142. North Street looking west, *c.*1929. Andrews' Library offering books and stationery, toys and fancy goods can be seen behind the Portslade Fruit Stores. Hart & Co.'s shop is on the right, advertising 'Furnishing Undertakers, Motor Hearse to any Distance' and 'Pianos for Sale'.

143. An advertisement for Hart & Co., published in 1922. The firm were auctioneers, removal contractors, furniture repositories and undertakers. They also had premises at Norway Street, Franklin Road and Carlton Terrace.

144. North Street used to be the main shopping thoroughfare in Portslade. This photograph, *c.*1907, shows how the street was lined with shops, very characteristic of Station Road/Boundary Road today. Andrews' Library is on the left, and on the far right is James Hopkins & Sons, grocers and agents for Gilbey's wines and spirits. The sign on the pavement advertises Gilbey's port. Low's chemist is next door and on the corner of East Street is the *Clarendon Arms* public house.

45. The shopfront of George Ariss at nos. 61 and 63 North Street, *c.*1907. Early closing in Portslade was on Wednesdays, with Mr. Ariss shutting his shop at two o'clock.

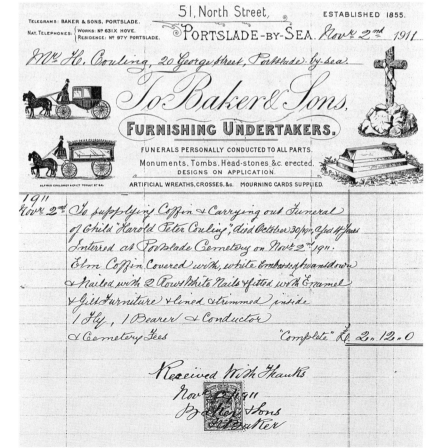

1911
Nov. 2nd To supplying Coffin & Carrying out Funeral
of Child "Harold Peter Couling", died October 30/p.m. Aged 4 years
Interred at Portslade Cemetery on Nov. 2nd 1911.
Elm Coffin Covered with white Embossed twansdown
& Nailed with 2 Rows White Nails & fitted with Enamel
& Gilt Furniture & lined & trimmed inside
1 Fly, 1 Bearer & Conductor
& Cemetery Fees   "Complete" £ 2 . 12 . 0

Received With Thanks
Nov 2 1911
Baker & Sons
S. Baker

146. A decorative invoice dated 2 November 1911, issued by Baker & Sons to Mr. Couling of George Street, Portslade, for the funeral of his son, Harold, aged four. George Street is situated off North Street but it is no longer residential.

147.   Station Road, *c*.1907. From the left, the shops are: Hardwick's (provisions); F. E. Kessell (tobacconist); E. W. Kippin (fruiterer); H. W. Tubb (photographer); Edward Clark (draper) and George Harwood (chemist). Huckles is pictured on the corner of Franklin Road with furniture being displayed on the pavement.

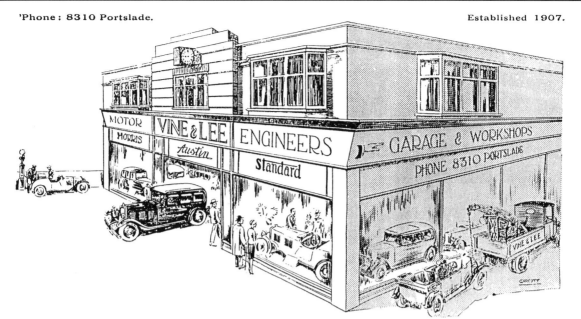

MOTOR
MORRIS
VINE & LEE
Austin
ENGINEERS
standard

GARAGE & WORKSHOPS
PHONE 8310 PORTSLADE

Proprietor : A. W. LEE, F.I.M.T., M.Inst.B.E.

Agents for MORRIS, AUSTIN, STANDARD, LANCHESTER, DAIMLER and HUMBER CARS.

Any make of car supplied. Your old car taken in part payment. TERMS ARRANGED.

Repairs carried out on the premises under the personal supervision of the Proprietor. Garage for 300 Cars.

148. An advertisement for Vine & Lee's garage in 1935. Established in 1907, Vine & Lee were situated, until 1974, where the Tesco store is today.

149. Boundary Road shops, *c.*1918. From the Portland Road end, the shops are Edward Taylor (grocer); George Barnes & Sons (butchers); Harry Greenfield (greengrocer); Henry Wingfield (stationer); James White (dairyman); Eli Andrews (fancy repositories); William Stanbridge (confectioner); E. Robins & Son Ltd. (wine and spirit merchants); A. E. Wilson (oilman) and Ethel Bacon (draper).

150. A 1935 advertisement for Huckles Ltd. Huckles were a long established firm of furniture retailers on the corner of Franklin Road and Station Road until their closure in 1988. The showroom now belongs to Advance Glass.

"The nicest shop in Portslade"
—says a Customer.

Where enormous stocks of reliable furnishings are available at reasonable prices, suitable for the home you live in. Agent for products of

BUOYANT
STAPLES
COMPACTUM
EWBANK

LIMITED

Managing Director: A. E. HUCKLE.

CORNER HOUSE : Telephone 8446

STATION ROAD
• PORTSLADE •

where thirty years ago was the entrance to Red House Farm.

151. A 1922 advertisement for John Glascock, stonemason, whose works in Victoria Road were 'one minute from Portslade station'.

152. Mr. Ernest Robinson and his family in 1924, outside their general store at no. 9 Elm Road.
His wife, Alice, stands in the doorway with daughters Grace and Dora, whilst son, Charles, holds the
barrow. In 1932, Alice took over the shop from her husband and ran it until 1971, when she declared
that the shop would close. Alice felt that she could not cope with decimalisation and retired at the
age of 87. The shop never reopened and has now been converted into a private house.

153. In addition to running the shop, Ernest Robinson had a furniture removal business and was also
a coal, coke and wood merchant. Christmas week 1926 saw a visit from Father Christmas with a tub
of 'Xmas Gifts' to give to the children.

Industry

154.   Electricity had been generated at the works in North Road, Brighton since 1891. The power station at Portslade opened on 16 June 1906 as, by this time, the North Road works had become inadequate. Over the years, the capacity of the Portslade plant increased and two large brick chimneys were added. The works later became known as 'Brighton A' when a second power station, 'Brighton B', was built at Southwick in 1952. March 1969 saw the start of 'Brighton A's shut down with closure of part of the works. Production finally stopped on 15 March 1976. The two brick chimneys were detonated on 12 June 1977, with the rest of the structure being demolished in May 1980.

155. Brighton and Hove General Gas Company's works at Portslade opened in 1871 and by 1885 were the sole manufacturer of gas to the area, following the closure of the works at Hove and Black Rock. The Portslade works were enlarged in the 1920s as a result of increased demand for gas supply. The retort house was built in 1954 and the high pressure reforming plant in 1965. Improvements were still being made in 1970 but the changeover to natural gas contributed to the works closure. Production stopped in April 1971 and the works finally closed on 22 May 1971. This photograph shows the gas works after closure and before demolition.

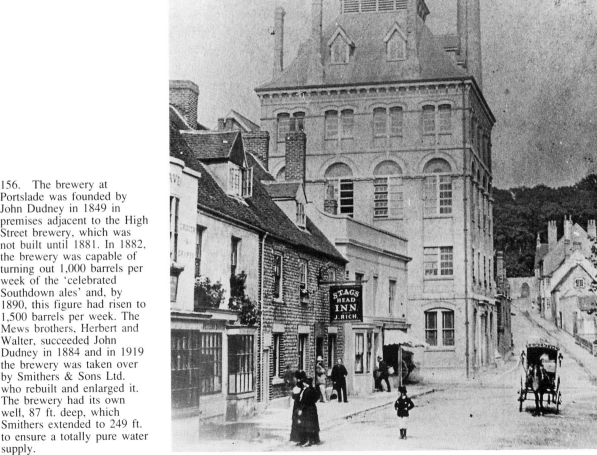

156. The brewery at Portslade was founded by John Dudney in 1849 in premises adjacent to the High Street brewery, which was not built until 1881. In 1882, the brewery was capable of turning out 1,000 barrels per week of the 'celebrated Southdown ales' and, by 1890, this figure had risen to 1,500 barrels per week. The Mews brothers, Herbert and Walter, succeeded John Dudney in 1884 and in 1919 the brewery was taken over by Smithers & Sons Ltd. who rebuilt and enlarged it. The brewery had its own well, 87 ft. deep, which Smithers extended to 249 ft. to ensure a totally pure water supply.

157. The ever increasing output of the brewery necessitated more improvements and modernisation. In 1922, the ornamental roof was removed and an upper storey added in the form of a water tank. The chimney was also subsequently altered. Smithers and Sons were brewers until 21 August 1930, and in 1933 the brewery was taken over by E. C. Stanford & Co. who owned it until 1937. This photograph, c.1939, shows the former brewery being used by Shepherd's Industries, a manufacturing company. Le Carbone took over the premises in 1947.

158. Detail on the base of the brewery chimney depicting hops and barley sheaves. 'A.D. 1881' denotes the year of construction, and 'D & S' stands for Dudney & Sons.

159.   The reservoir and water works at Mile Oak, shown working. This Victorian pumping station was built in 1900 and consisted of two Fleming & Ferguson 130 h.p. triple compound steam engines; *Reeves* and *Kelly*. The water works were owned by Victor Puttock, and Thomas Puttock was the engineer. The pumping station was demolished in 1961 when a new building was erected to house an electric pump.

160.   John Eede Butt & Sons were timber importers with sawing mills and slate yards at Baltic Wharf, Wellington Road. They were also proprietors of the Norfolk Steam Sawing, Planing and Moulding Mills at Littlehampton, and of the Trafalgar Lane Steam Mills, Brighton. The timber yard is today operated by Travis Perkins.

WE MUST HAVE FRYCO AT THE PARTY!

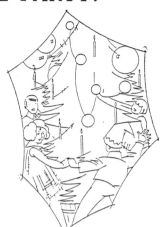

Christmas once again — the season of fun and festivity —when the children really come into their own.

There are parties to be thought of now, and the hostess, looking for something new, should try Fryco Non-Alcoholic Wines— she will be delighted with their delicious flavour and aroma. The children love Fryco; it's good for them too, for it is made from the highest quality ingredients.

Why not try a bottle to-day?

Your grocer stocks Fryco.

FRYCO

Sole Manufacturers: NON-ALCOHOLIC FRUIT WINES & CORDIALS.
R. FRY & CO., Ltd., Portslade, near Brighton.

161. An advertisement for 'Fryco' published in the *Brighton & Hove Herald*, December 1932. R. Fry & Co. Ltd. were manufacturers of non-alcoholic wines, mineral water and soft drinks whose extensive premises were in Middle Street, Brighton until they moved to Victoria Road, Portslade in 1930. The business was taken over by the Schweppes Group in 1961 and the brand name 'Fryco' was sold.

162. An advertisement for Ronuk polish which appeared in the 1920s. Ronuk Ltd. was registered as a company on 2 November 1896, although the product had been marketed considerably earlier. The famous polish was invented by the father of Thomas Horace Fowler, managing director of Ronuk Ltd., and was known as Fowler's Wax Composition. Ronuk Ltd. began production from the ground floor of a building in Providence Place, Brighton but its popularity and growth necessitated a move to larger premises in Portslade in 1902. Ronuk Ltd. established their first factory just off Victoria Road, and new blocks and offices were built around it as the company expanded. The company also had its own private railway siding. Several factors contributed to Ronuk's closure in the late 1950s. Advancement in the industry meant that by this time their processes were outdated and spray polish was becoming fashionable. The Metal Box factory, which had been manufacturing the tins for Ronuk, went over to plastic, and the closure of the railway sidings meant that there was no other way for the goods to be transported.

RONUK RONUK RONUK

Sing a song of RONUK.
Housewives all agree,
Here's the stuff to make your floors
Shine continually.
When the door is opened
Brightness meets your sight,
What a highly polished home
To welcome you at night!

RONUK

FLOOR POLISH

POLISHES. PRESERVES. PURIFIES.

For your Furniture, use RONUK FURNITURE CREAM.

When buying RONUK, ask to see that wonderful labour-saving device, the RONUK HOME POLISHER.

Sold Everywhere. Manufactured by RONUK, Ltd., Portslade, Sussex.

163. A decorative billhead from 1928, promoting Ronuk polish. The name 'Ronuk' derived from an anglicised version of an eastern word meaning 'splendour' and 'brilliance'.

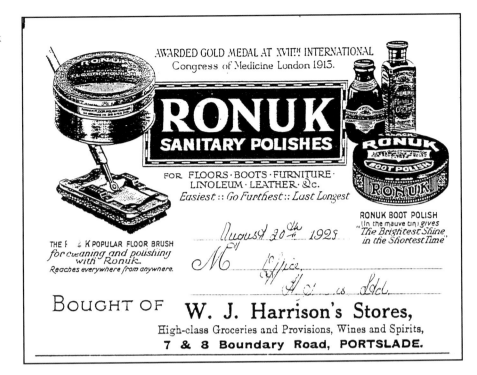

AWARDED GOLD MEDAL AT XVIIᵗʰ INTERNATIONAL
Congress of Medicine London 1913.

RONUK
SANITARY POLISHES

FOR FLOORS · BOOTS · FURNITURE ·
LINOLEUM · LEATHER · &c.
Easiest :: Go Furthest :: Last Longest

RONUK BOOT POLISH
"In the mauve tin; gives
*"The Brightest Shine
in the Shortest Time"*

THE RONUK POPULAR FLOOR BRUSH
*for cleaning and polishing
with Ronuk.
Reaches everywhere from anywhere.*

August 20th 1928

BOUGHT OF **W. J. Harrison's Stores,**
High-class Groceries and Provisions, Wines and Spirits,
7 & 8 Boundary Road, PORTSLADE.

164. Tate's Southern Cross Laundry was situated on the Old Shoreham Road, at the corner of Foredown Drive. It was built in 1900 for Alfred Tate, the proprietor, and boasted 'good open drying ground'. The claim is illustrated in this view of the laundry's drying ground, where the linen is being pegged out. The laundry closed in the late 1940s, and houses in Foredown Drive were built on the old drying ground. The former laundry building, then the factory of Shoreham Moulders Ltd., was destroyed by fire on 29 March 1954.

THE SOUTHERN CROSS LAUNDRY,
OLD SHOREHAM ROAD, PORTSLADE.

NAT. TELE.
No. **95 x.**

CLEANING
and
DYEING ..

*of every
description.*

A Post Card
will bring
a Van to
your door.

· THE DRYING GROUND.

Modern Portslade

165.   Portslade Health Centre was built on the site of the old St Andrew's vicarage. A new building was considered necessary when the surgery at no. 245 New Church Road, Hove became too small. Here, the practice operated from the ground floor of a Victorian house, having just two consulting rooms, outside toilets and a small waiting room. The New Church Road surgery closed on 30 April 1982 after 80 years. The new purpose-built surgery, with clinic facilities, pharmacy and six consulting rooms each with its own examination room, was officially opened on 15 June 1982 by Mrs. Julia Cumberledge, Chairman of Brighton Health Authority.

166.   Southern Sound Radio, now Southern FM, opened on 29 August 1983 at Radio House, Franklin Road, the redesigned premises of the former Rothbury cinema, built in 1934. The station broadcasts contemporary 'classic hits' on 103.5 FM, covering both East and West Sussex, and was the first of six commercial radio stations to be operated by Southern Radio Plc., the fourth largest commercial radio group in the United Kingdom.

167.   Station Road is now the main shopping thoroughfare of Portslade. The majority of the old houses have been knocked down or converted into shops, and major retailers such as Tesco are taking advantage of this prime position. Tesco was built on the site of the old Vine & Lee garage and the store opened on 17 February 1981. The name Tesco a fusion of the names of its founders, Mr. Cohen and his wife, Tessa.

168.   The Rivervale premises were originally built for Prestwich Motors in 1968 on former British Rail freight sidings. Originally agents for Volkswagen, Prestwich later took on Datsun and Mercedes-Benz. Rivervale, part of Endeavour Holdings, purchased the premises in 1983, and relinquished the Datsun franchise to concentrate on Mercedes-Benz. The showroom was extended in 1985 which included the addition of first-floor offices.

169.   A new showroom and offices for Rivervale's Porsche franchise opened in 1990, this being the adjacent round building. The recession meant that in January 1992 the Porsche franchise was moved in with Mercedes-Benz and the round building became WestHove Nissan.

170. Building commenced on the houses in Hamilton Close in 1991. Built by the Chichester Diocesan Housing Association in conjunction with Hove Borough Council, the estate is named after Portslade councillor and former Mayor of Hove, Leslie Hamilton.

171. The houses at Benfield Heights were built by Persimmon Homes on the site of the old Foredown Isolation Hospital. Building started in early spring 1989 and the first homes were completed around July the same year. The development is enclosed on three sides by the original flint boundary wall and the trees carry a preservation order.

172. Plaque denoting the year Foredown Isolation Hospital opened, removed from the old administration building and inset into the wall at Benfield Heights. The flats, Pickford Court, were built where the administration building once stood.

173. Appleyard's was built on land formerly owned by Southdown Motor Services. In 1986, the Southdown group split up to become Brighton & Hove Bus Company and Stagecoach, and the works at Portslade became Southdown Engineering. The Appleyard Group purchased the land in 1988 and Southdown Engineering leased part of it back. Appleyard's demolished the remainder of the old Southdown site in order to build their showroom, which opened in June 1989 as Endeavours. In 1991, the Appleyard Group sold Endeavours and the building closed for 18 months before reopening as Seat dealers on 17 October 1992.

174. Established in 1919, Tates are a family-run business, synonymous with the motor trade in Portslade and the Brighton area, having a Citroen franchise on the Old Shoreham Road, Fiat franchise in Church Road, and sales centres for conservatories and caravans in Trafalgar Road. Building commenced on the new Fiat showroom in spring 1993. Built on the site of the old scout hut on the corner of St Andrew's Road, the showroom was officially opened on 2 October 1993.

Bibliography

Banks, B., *Portslade Brief History*, *c.*1980

Bateley, Capt. I., 'Historical Notes', manuscript

Blaauw, W., 'Wakehurst, Slaugham & Gravetye', *Sussex Archaeological Collections*, Vol.10, 1858

Blencoe, R. W., 'Extracts from the Parish Registers', *Sussex Archaeological Collections*, Vol.4, 1851

Carder, T., *The Encyclopaedia of Brighton*, 1990

Dale, A., *Brighton Churches*, 1989

Dunning, J., *The Roman Road to Portslade*, 1925

Fermer, H., 'Foredown Isolation Hospital', *Sussex Industrial History*, Issue 20, 1990

Gray, J. S., *Brighton Between the Wars*, 1976

Holden, E. W., 'Excavations at the Deserted Medieval Village of Hangleton', *Sussex Archaeological Collections*, Vol.101, 1963

Holden, E. W., 'Port's Road: The Ancient Road of Portslade', *Sussex Archaeological Collections*, Vol.114, 1976

Horsfield, T. W., *History, Antiquities and Topography of the County of Sussex*, 1835

Howard Turner, J. T., *The London, Brighton & South Coast Railway 2: Establishment and Growth*, 1978

Middleton, J., *A History of St Nicolas' School*, 1990

Morris, C., *British Bus Systems No.6: Southdown*, 1985

Morris, J. (ed.), *History from the Sources: Domesday Book—Sussex*, 1976

Portslade History Group, *The History of Portslade*, 1977

Roberts, J., *British Bus & Trolley Bus Systems No.4: Brighton, Hove and District*, 1984

Simmons, D. A., *Schweppes: The First 200 Years*, 1983

Sussex Notes and Queries, Vol.7, 1938-39

The Victoria County History of Sussex, Vol.7, 1940

Brighton & Hove Herald

Evening Argus

Kelly's Directory of Sussex

Sussex County Magazine

Sussex Daily News